SPIRITUAL WARFARE

fighting the good
fight of faith

Brian Brodersen

Spiritual Warfare
Fighting the Good Fight of Faith

Copyright © 2009 by Brian Brodersen

Published by Back To Basics
a resource ministry of Calvary Chapel of Costa Mesa
3800 South Fairview Rd.
Santa Ana, CA 92704

First printing, 2004
Second printing, 2006
Third printing, 2008
Fourth printing, 2009

ISBN 978-1-93166-772-2

Printed in the United States of America

CONTENTS

PREFACE

As the dark night of human history moves closer and closer to its climactic end, it becomes more obviously the history of a great cosmic battle between good and evil. But not just a battle between good and evil in the philosophical sense, but more specifically, a battle between God and the devil. A battle between the servants of Jesus Christ and the invisible forces of Satan. A battle that is, in essence, a spiritual battle. A battle that a Christian, by his or her very relationship with Christ, is unavoidably drawn into. A battle that is not observed with the physical eye nor fought with weapons crafted by men, but a battle fought in the realm of the Spirit through spiritual means such as prayer, the proclamation of God's truth, and holy living.

Spiritual Warfare was written to heighten the Christian's awareness of this spiritual battle and its reality in our daily lives. It was also written with the hope of bringing a biblical balance to a vitally important, but often misunderstood subject.

My prayer is that God will use the truths herein to enlighten and strengthen His people in the fight of faith.

Brian Brodersen
Costa Mesa, California

1 THE BATTLE

> Put on the whole armor of God, that you
> may be able to stand against the wiles of the
> devil. For we do not wrestle against flesh
> and blood, but against principalities, against
> powers, against the rulers of the darkness of
> this age, against spiritual hosts of wickedness
> in the heavenly places.
>
> *Ephesians 6:11–12*

Wouldn't it be nice if the Christian life was simply believing in Jesus and living happily ever after?
But anyone who has sought to seriously follow the
Lord has found it to be otherwise. Jesus promised His followers that tribulation and opposition
would mark life in this world. The primary source
of that opposition is the devil and a multitude of
wicked spirits who form a united front against the
kingdom of God.

The enemy's opposition is evident in a mil-
lion different situations, but they're all connected.
We see it in everything from bombed churches

in Pakistan and Indonesia; to the murder of kid-napped missionaries in the Philippines; to the imprisonment of church leaders in Communist China; to the United States judicial system's stand against the display of the Ten Commandments or a cross on public property; to the media's constant assault upon the church and biblical standards of morality; to the scientific community's irrational hatred of the idea of divine creation as an explanation for the origins of life; to the persecution that comes on the job or from family members; to the confusion and doubt that sometimes clouds our minds as we attempt to study the Bible; to the distractions that bombard us while we're trying to pray; to the fear that seizes us when opportunities to share our faith arise; to the battle that often ensues as we attempt to gather for fellowship.

Now, I am certain that every Christian has faced this opposition, some more intensely than others. Yet, I am also certain that many have not realized that these difficulties are part of a fierce spiritual battle.

One of Satan's most effective strategies is to keep us ignorant of the existence of this spiritual warfare. He disguises himself so well that we do not recognize what is actually taking place. To paraphrase C. S. Lewis, the devils hail with delight the materialist who disbelieves in their existence.[1] Although Lewis's statement might not apply to any of us directly because we are Christians, not materialists, it does apply in that we often live in oblivion to the spiritual realm that surrounds us.

None of us wants to be defeated by this opposition, so an introduction to the reality of spiritual warfare will help us on our way to the victory our Lord promises in this battle.

THE OPPOSITION

First let's consider the inspiration behind the conflict: the devil and his angels. Who is the devil? Is he a real entity or just a mythological figure?

The Bible teaches that the devil is a real person, a spirit being who was originally God's most glorious creature, but by an act of rebellion has become God's archenemy (Isaiah 14; Ezekiel 28). The Bible tells us that he is incredibly powerful, exceedingly intelligent, and immeasurably evil. Scripture also teaches that he is perpetually at war with God and His people. He is the commander and chief of a multitude of creatures similar to himself. Paul refers to this army of evil creatures as "principalities and powers, the rulers of the darkness of this world, spiritual wickedness in high places" (see Ephesians 6:12). All of these indicate organized opposition.

By way of analogy, consider the Roman Empire. Caesar sat in Rome and made policy based upon his counsel with the senate. The senators would pass the decisions of the counsel down to the governors and rulers who would then implement their decisions. Likewise, within the kingdom of Satan there are those high-ranking officials making policy and those lower-ranking representatives that implement policy.

One of Daniel's prophecies gives us insight into the kingdom of Satan.

> In the third year of Cyrus king of Persia, a revelation was given to Daniel (who was called Belteshazzar). Its message was true and it concerned a great war. The understanding of the message came to him in a vision.
>
> At that time I, Daniel, mourned for three weeks. I ate no choice food; no meat or wine touched my lips; and I used no lotions at all until the three weeks were over.
>
> On the twenty-fourth day of the first month, as I was standing on the bank of the great

river, the Tigris, I looked up and there before me was a man dressed in linen, with a belt of the finest gold around his waist. His body was like chrysolite, his face like lightning, his eyes like flaming torches, his arms and legs like the gleam of burnished bronze, and his voice like the sound of a multitude.

I, Daniel, was the only one who saw the vision; the men with me did not see it, but such terror overwhelmed them that they fled and hid themselves. So I was left alone, gazing at this great vision; I had no strength left, my face turned deathly pale and I was helpless. Then I heard him speaking, and as I listened to him, I fell into a deep sleep, my face to the ground.

A hand touched me and set me trembling on my hands and knees. He said, "Daniel, you who are highly esteemed, consider carefully the words I am about to speak to you, and stand up, for I have now been sent to you." And when he said this to me, I stood up trembling.

Then he continued, "Do not be afraid, Daniel. Since the first day that you set your mind to gain understanding and to humble yourself before your God, your words were heard, and I have come in response to them. *But the prince of the Persian kingdom resisted me twenty-one days.* Then Michael, one of the chief princes, came to help me, because I was detained there with the king of Persia. Now I have come to explain to you what will happen to your people in the future, for the vision concerns a time yet to come."

Daniel 10:1–14 NIV, italics added

Notice what the angel said: "But the prince of the Persian kingdom resisted me twenty-one days." Cyrus was the king of Persia at that time, yet he most certainly was not the one resisting this angelic messenger. The reference is to the spiritual power behind the Persian Empire. Similar accounts appear in Isaiah 14 and Ezekiel 28 where the prophets are prophesying against the kings of Babylon and Tyre. As they are prophesying, suddenly and without explanation, they begin to address the spiritual power behind these earthly rulers.

These passages, among many others, should undoubtedly lead us to conclude that the world we live in is not solely the material world it appears to be. There is also a spiritual dimension, and the world is actually governed by "wicked spirits in high places." It is imperative that we recognize this biblical truth.

Let's look at another example from the New Testament of this invisible kingdom. Do you remember when the Lord was being tempted? Satan showed Him all the kingdoms of the world in all their glory and said to Him, "All this authority I will give You, and their glory; for this has been delivered to me, and I give it to whomever I wish" (Luke 4:6). Jesus neither disputed Satan's claim of authority over the kingdoms of the world nor his ability to give them to whomever he wished. In fact, Jesus affirmed Satan's claim when He later referred to him as "the ruler of this world" (John 14:30).

Understanding these biblical facts is vital to our spiritual well being. Tragically, many Christians have been seduced into thinking the way the average person thinks—regarding everything as merely a result of natural processes. However, Paul says, "We wrestle not against flesh and blood." We as Christians need to remember that.

THE CONFLICT

The next thing we need to consider is the intimate

nature of the conflict indicated by the term *wrestle*. There are really two aspects to spiritual warfare. There is the general sense in which the collective forces of God are battling the collective forces of Satan. Then there is also a very personal aspect in which you and I are engaged in hand-to-hand combat with demonic spirits. It's a wrestling match. It's intimate. It's personal. It's deadly. As a Christian, you are being studied, stalked, and assaulted regularly. Failure to realize this can result in your becoming a casualty in the conflict.

Maybe at this point, you're thinking, "Wait a minute, aren't you going a bit overboard? What do you mean, I'm being studied, stalked, and assaulted by demons? You sound like a fanatic!"

I can assure you that I am not being fanatical, but rather scriptural. I'm simply stating what the Bible teaches generally and what it refers to specifically in the case of Job, among others.

> One day the angels came to present themselves before the LORD, and Satan also came with them. The LORD said to Satan, "Where have you come from?" Satan answered the LORD, "From roaming through the earth and going back and forth in it."

> Then the LORD said to Satan, "Have you considered my servant Job? There is no one on earth like him; he is blameless and upright, a man who fears God and shuns evil."
>
> "Does Job fear God for nothing?" Satan replied. "Have you not put a hedge around him and his household and everything he has?"
>
> *Job 1:6–10 NIV*

You see, Satan had studied Job. He had stalked him. Very shortly, he would assault him. Satan's tactics have not changed over the centuries. You and I are subject to the same kinds of attacks Job experienced. My intention is not to inspire paranoia, but rather to help you see the world and your own personal experiences through a biblical lens. Christians, today more than ever, need a biblical worldview, one that includes a belief in and an understanding of the spiritual realm.

THE BATTLE IS THE LORD'S!

Now that we have established the reality of spiritual warfare, we need to learn how to survive in this invisible battle. The first thing to remember is that "the battle is the Lord's" (1 Samuel 17:47);

therefore, we must be "strong in the Lord and in the power of His might" (Ephesians 6:10). We have no natural power with which to defeat the forces of darkness. If I am to be victorious, I must draw my strength from the Lord. It was this acknowledgement that gave victory to men like David and Jehoshaphat.

When David faced Goliath, he made it clear that he stood in God's strength.

> Then David said to the Philistine, "You come to me with a sword, with a spear, and with a javelin. But I come to you in the name of the LORD of hosts, the God of the armies of Israel, whom you have defied. This day the LORD will deliver you into my hand, and I will strike you and take your head from you. And this day I will give the carcasses of the camp of the Philistines to the birds of the air and the wild beasts of the earth, that all the earth may know that there is a God in Israel. Then all this assembly shall know that the LORD does not save with sword and spear; for the battle is the LORD's, and He will give you into our hands."
>
> *1 Samuel 17:45–47*

Likewise, when Jehoshaphat cried to the Lord for deliverance from his enemies, the prophet Jahaziel responded:

> Listen, all you of Judah and you inhabitants of Jerusalem, and you, King Jehoshaphat! Thus says the LORD to you: "Do not be afraid nor dismayed because of this great multitude, for the battle is not yours, but God's."
>
> *2 Chronicles 20:15*

It is critical that we remember this lest we be overcome with fear and discouragement.

THE WEAPONS OF OUR WARFARE

Another important truth to remember is that "the weapons of our warfare are not carnal but mighty in God" (2 Corinthians 10:4). The word *carnal* is the antithesis of *spiritual* and refers to that which is merely human. Apart from the power of God, all of our energies combined are to no avail against the power of darkness. Since we are in a spiritual battle, we need spiritual weapons. That is exactly what God has supplied us with—"weapons … mighty in God for pulling down strongholds, casting down arguments and every high thing that exalts itself against the knowledge of God." Weapons mighty in God! The word *mighty* can be translated "dynamically powerful." God has supplied us with more than we need for victory. We just have to tap into that which is already available to us.

What are the "weapons" God has given us? They are simply prayer, the Word of God, and worship. We must be thoroughly immersed in these if we are going to successfully fight the "good fight of faith." Later, we'll take an in-depth look at these weapons that are "mighty in God," but for now, let's move on to an in-depth consideration of the enemy.

2

THE GOD OF THIS AGE

> Now there was a day when the sons of God came to present themselves before the LORD, and Satan also came among them. And the LORD said to Satan, "From where do you come?"
>
> So Satan answered the LORD and said, "From going to and fro on the earth, and from walking back and forth on it."
>
> *Job 1:6–7*

From this passage, we see that our enemy, Satan, is indeed alive and well on planet Earth. Therefore, the question is: What is he doing? The answer: a whole lot more than most people realize. Let's look at some of the devil's activities in the world.

THE NATURAL REALM

First, we will consider the devil's activity in the realm of nature. The Bible teaches that the devil has a certain degree of power over nature. Consequently, many of those things that we would glibly refer to as "natural disasters" or "acts of God" are actually manifestations of Satan's work. Now I'm not saying that every catastrophe is the result of satanic activity, but when you consider the death and destruction that result from these calamities and the subsequent blame that is generally placed upon God, it is valid to assume that many of these events are satanically orchestrated. At the very least, Satan attempts to manipulate "natural disasters" to destroy, discourage, and defeat the work of God in the world.

A biblical basis for this view comes once again from the book of Job.

> Then the LORD said to Satan, "Have you considered My servant Job, that there is none like him on the earth, a blameless and upright man, one who fears God and shuns evil?"

> So Satan answered the LORD and said, "Does Job fear God for nothing? Have You not made a hedge around him, around his household, and around all that he has on every side? You have blessed the work of his hands, and his possessions have increased in

the land. But now, stretch out Your hand and touch all that he has, and he will surely curse You to Your face!"

And the LORD said to Satan, "Behold, all that he has is in your power; only do not lay a hand on his person." So Satan went out from the presence of the LORD.

Now there was a day when his sons and daughters were eating and drinking wine in their oldest brother's house; and a messenger came to Job and said, "The oxen were plowing and the donkeys feeding beside them, when the Sabeans raided them and took them away—indeed they have killed the servants with the edge of the sword; and I alone have escaped to tell you!"

While he was still speaking, another also came and said, "The fire of God fell from heaven and burned up the sheep and the servants, and consumed them; and I alone have escaped to tell you!"

While he was still speaking, another also came and said, "The Chaldeans formed three bands, raided the camels and took them away, yes, and killed the servants with the edge of the sword; and I alone have escaped to tell you!"

While he was still speaking, another also came and said, "Your sons and daughters were eating and drinking wine in their oldest brother's house, and suddenly a great wind came from across the wilderness and struck the four corners of the house, and it fell on the young people, and they are dead; and I alone have escaped to tell you!"

Job 1:8–19

Here is a classic example of Satan manipulating nature in his war against God. The fire that fell from the sky and destroyed the flocks and the servants and the wind that caused the house to collapse on Job's children, killing them, were a direct result of the devil's activity. Yet, the messenger referred to the fire as "the fire of God." Satan destroys lives and then seeks to put the blame on God. He still does this today.

Victims of earthquakes, fires, floods, or storms will often imply that God is somehow responsible for their misery. Reports in newspapers and on TV usually echo the sentiment that God is somehow to blame. Though outside the realm of "natural disaster," this kind of accusation was seen and heard frequently following the terrorist attacks upon

New York City and Washington DC. As was the case in the life of Job, I believe the real culprit in those attacks was the devil.

The word *devil* means "slanderer or accuser." Satan will stir up the forces of nature, bring death and destruction, and then accuse God of being responsible for the whole mess. The tragedy is that most people believe him. Am I saying that earthquakes, floods, and hurricanes are the work of Satan? My answer: not always, but perhaps more often than we think. When you consider Satan's goal—to kill and destroy—"natural disasters" provide for him an excellent arena in which to work.

HUMAN AFFAIRS

But Satan doesn't stop there! He is also busy at work in the affairs of men. Whether it's international politics, the media, academia, the entertainment industry, or the fads and fashions of the world, his influence is undeniable. Paul referred to Satan as "the prince of the power of the air, the spirit who now works in the sons of disobedience" (Ephesians 2:2).

From evolutionary theory to Marxist philosophy, from racial prejudice to multiculturalism, from the sexual revolution to gay marriages, from broken homes to the epidemic of violent crime, from alcoholism to drug addiction—Satan's work is evident. The hatred and violence, the death and destruction, and the pain and the misery from the beginning of history until today can all, to a large degree, be attributed to the activity of the devil.

The personality, purpose, and power of the devil were clearly revealed in the person of Adolf Hitler and the events that surrounded his attempt to rule the world. If you want an up-close-and-personal look at what the devil is like, just consider the actions of Hitler's Third Reich and the atrocities of the Second World War, especially the attempted extermination of the Jewish people.

The Communists provide another example of the true nature of Satan. Think of the millions of people murdered under the radical antichrist spirit that is so prevalent among the adherents of Marxism. The late Richard Wurmbrand, who suffered immense persecution under the Communist regime in Romania, wrote a book entitled *Marx and Satan* in which he documented Marx's early involvement in Satanism.

Satan is not to be regarded lightly; rather, he is

a horrific beast who is set on destroying as many people as possible.

More recently, Satan has been expressing himself through Muslim extremists and their murderous rampages against all those who disagree with their fanatical views. His influence is especially obvious in the militant anti-Israel, anti-Christian rhetoric coming out of certain segments of the Islamic community.

Truly, as the apostle John said, "The whole world lies under the sway of the wicked one" (1 John 5:19).

FALSE RELIGION

Another manifestation of the devil's activity is false religion. This is Satan's masterpiece and perhaps his greatest means of influence. It is also his most deadly weapon because it is aimed directly at men's souls. The ultimate goal of the devil is to keep a human soul from the salvation that is available in Christ, and he will do anything in his power—even to the point of encouraging religious devotion—to obtain the desired results.

The apostle Paul said, "For Satan himself

transforms himself into an angel of light" (2 Corinthians 11:14). He has kept multitudes of people blinded to the truth through false religious systems. As Paul also said:

> If our gospel is veiled, it is veiled to those who are perishing, whose minds the god of this age has blinded, who do not believe, lest the light of the gospel of the glory of Christ, who is the image of God, should shine on them.

2 Corinthians 4:3–4

In reality, the so-called great religions of the world are nothing less than satanic counterfeits intended to destroy men's souls eternally. I know that might sound extreme to some, but if you take the Bible seriously, that is the only conclusion that can be drawn. Some insist that all religions essentially teach the same thing and all are equally valid. Yet, a simple comparison between Hinduism and Christianity, for example, shows the fallacy of this position.

Hinduism teaches that there are millions of gods, and Christianity insists that there is only one God. A comparison of Buddhism and Christianity shows the same thing. Buddhism does not involve belief in God at all; it is inherently atheistic. Islam denies the core Christian belief that Jesus Christ is God's only begotten Son. The pseudo-Christian cults like the Mormons and Jehovah's Witnesses would also be examples of satanic counterfeits.

But the devil's activity is not limited only to these other religions. We also see it in the church. Many in the mainline Protestant denominations have actually left the faith. They no longer believe that Jesus Christ is God in the flesh or that He was born of a virgin. They no longer believe that He died an atoning death on the Cross or that He literally rose bodily from the dead. They don't believe that the Bible is the Word of God. One wonders why they call themselves "Christian." They reject outright most of what the Bible teaches.

Then finally, much of Roman Catholicism would have to be included in this same category for its many aberrant beliefs and practices. Everything from the Mass to the pope, to the priesthood, to the supposed mediation of Mary and the saints is contrary to the simple message of salvation presented in the Scriptures. The Roman Catholic Church's claim that it is the "one true church" is indefensible both biblically and historically.[2]

Satan is indeed active! He is manipulating the forces of nature and bringing disaster upon men, he is at work in society oppressing people through various philosophies that lead to tyranny and war, and he's busy spreading false religion that he might steal men's souls and rob them of eternal life.

As we gain a greater awareness of Satan's activities in the world, may it provoke us to a greater use of the mighty weapons of prayer and the proclamation of the gospel. It's through prayer that catastrophe can be turned into an opportunity for God to work. It's through both prayer and proclamation that God intervenes in the affairs of men by pouring out His Spirit and bringing about radical change. The Reformation and the Great Awakenings are good examples of God using adverse conditions to accomplish His work. It's through the proclamation of the gospel that men are freed from the blinding effects of false religion and brought to a saving knowledge of Christ.

Any good military strategist makes it a point to know the strategy of his enemy. The more familiar we are with the devil's schemes, the more effective we will be in overcoming him and helping others to do so as well. Now, let's proceed to still another aspect of the devil's activity, "the wiles of the devil."

3

THE WILES OF THE DEVIL

> Put on the whole armor of God, that you
> may be able to stand against the wiles of the
> devil … above all, taking the shield of faith
> with which you will be able to quench all the
> fiery darts of the wicked one.
>
> *Ephesians 6:11, 16*

The "wiles of the devil" and the "fiery darts of the wicked one" cover a broad range of activity but no doubt include Satan's attack upon our mind and emotions. Experiences such as condemnation, doubt, fear, evil thoughts, and depression emanate from his attacks. Now, I do not claim to understand how it is that Satan can access our mind and emotions, but that he can is clear both from Scripture and from the testimony of many of God's servants throughout the long history of the church. Let's consider two examples of "the wiles of the devil," one from Scripture and one from church history.

The first involves the apostle Peter and is recorded in Matthew 16. Jesus asks the disciples, "Who do you say that I am?" Simon Peter answers, saying, "You are the Christ, the Son of the living God." Jesus commends him for his response, "Blessed are you Simon, Bar-Jonah, for flesh and blood has not revealed this to you, but My Father who is in heaven."

Then as Jesus proceeds to tell them about His coming rejection by the leaders at Jerusalem and His subsequent death on the Cross, Peter, well-meaning but misguided, takes Jesus aside and begins to rebuke Him, saying, "Far be it from You, Lord; this shall not happen to You!"

Jesus turns and says to Peter, "Get behind Me, Satan! You are an offense to Me, for you are not mindful of the things of God, but the things of men." Jesus' response to Peter illustrates my point. In the first instance, Peter's mind was influenced by the Lord. A few minutes later Peter was under the influence of Satan and his thoughts were satanically inspired.

The second striking example of the enemy's attack on the mind of a believer is seen in the life of John Bunyan, author of *The Pilgrim's Progress*.

Describing his experience in the book *Grace Abounding,* he writes:

> For about the space of a month …, a very great storm came down upon me, which handled me twenty times worse than all I had met with before; it came stealing upon me, now by one piece, then by another; first, all my comfort was taken from me, then darkness seized upon me, after which, whole floods of blasphemies, both against God, Christ, and the Scriptures, were poured upon my spirit, to my great confusion and astonishment. These blasphemous thoughts were such as also stirred up questions in me, against the very being of God, and of his only beloved Son; as, whether there were, in truth, a God, or Christ, or no? and whether the holy Scriptures were not rather a fable, and cunning story, than the holy and pure Word of God?
>
> The tempter would also much assault me with this, how can you tell but that the [Muslims] had as good Scriptures to prove their [Mohammed] the Saviour, as we have to prove our Jesus is? And, could I think, that so many ten thousands, in so many countries and kingdoms, should be without the knowledge of the right way to heaven; if there were indeed

a heaven, and that we only, who live in a corner of the earth, should alone be blessed therewith? Every one … [thinks] his own religion [right], both Jews and [Muslims], and Pagans! and [what] if all our faith, and Christ, and Scriptures, should be [the same thing] too?

Sometimes I have endeavoured to argue against these suggestions, and to set some of the sentences of blessed Paul against them; but, alas! I quickly felt, when I [did this], such arguings as these would return again upon me, though we made so great a matter of Paul, and of his words, [how do I know that Paul himself was not a deceiver and out to destroy his fellow men?]

These suggestions, with many other which at this time I may not, nor dare not utter, neither by word nor pen, did make such a seizure upon my spirit, and did so [overwhelm] my heart, both with their number, continuance, and fiery force, that I felt as if there were nothing else but these from morning to night within me; and as though, indeed, there could be room for nothing else; and also concluded, that God had, in very wrath to my soul, given me up unto them, to be carried away with them, as with a mighty whirlwind.

Only by the distaste that they gave unto my spirit, I felt there was something in me, that refused to embrace them. But this consideration I then only had, when God [gave me brief moments of relief], otherwise the noise, and strength, and force of these temptations, would drown and overflow; and as it were bury all such thoughts or the remembrance of any such thing. While I was in this temptation, I should often find my mind suddenly put upon it, to curse and swear, or to speak some grievous thing against God, or Christ his Son, and of the Scriptures.

Now I thought, surely I am possessed of the devil; at other times again, I thought I should be bereft of my wits; for instead of [praising] and magnifying God the Lord with others, if I have but heard him spoken of, presently some most horrible blasphemous thought or other would bolt out of my heart against him; so that whether I did think that God was, or again did think there were no such thing; no love, nor peace, nor gracious disposition could I feel within me.

These things did sink me into very deep despair; for I concluded, that such things could not possibly be found amongst them that loved God. I often, when these temptations have been with force upon me, did compare myself in the case of such a child, whom some [abductor had by force taken up and carried from family], friend and country; kick sometimes I did, and also scream and cry; but yet I was as bound in the wings of the temptation, and the wind would carry me away. I thought also of Saul, and of the evil spirit that did possess him; and did greatly fear that my condition was the same with that of his (1 Samuel 16:14).

In these days, when I have heard others talk of what was the sin against the Holy Ghost, then would the tempter so provoke me to desire to sin that sin, that I was as if I could not, must not, neither should be quiet until I had committed that; now, no sin would serve but that; if it were to be committed by speaking of such a word, then I have been as if my mouth would have spoken that word, whether I would or [not]; and in so strong a measure was this temptation upon me, that often I have been ready to [clasp] my hand under my chin, to hold my mouth from opening; and to that end also I have had thoughts at other times, to leap with my head downward, into some hole, to keep my mouth from speaking.[3]

What a vivid description of the kind of brutal warfare that we sometimes experience as God's servants! More than a single "fiery dart," Bunyan was assaulted with a continuous barrage of them. But he is not alone in this experience, for though we might not like to admit it, many of us have faced similar attacks.

Having established that the enemy frequently attacks our mind and emotions, we will now take a closer look at some of the "wiles of the devil" so that we can avoid being ensnared by them.

CONDEMNATION

A common tactic of the devil is to make you feel cut off from God's love and forgiveness. This occurs most often after some failure on your part. Maybe you did something that you knew you shouldn't have done or you didn't do something that you knew you should have done. That's when condemnation usually strikes. However, it is important to distinguish between conviction and condemnation. *Conviction* is a legitimate work of the Holy Spirit that produces guilt over our sins, which then leads us to the Cross to receive forgiveness. *Condemnation* produces guilt and leaves its victim with a sense of hopelessness.

The devil might suggest that God is finished with you by saying, "You've gone too far this time." He implies that forgiveness is no longer available. You might even have overwhelming feelings that God has abandoned you and that He no longer loves you. All of this is typical of the "fiery darts of the wicked one." These darts of the enemy can only be fended off by taking up the shield of faith—which is the Word of God. The power of condemnation lies in Satan's ability to deceive us into thinking that God is the one condemning us. After all, if God is against us, who can be for us? What a vile distortion of the truth!

In Romans 8:1 Paul says, "There is therefore now no condemnation to those who are in Christ Jesus. …" Then in verse 31 he says, "If God is for us, who can be against us?" In verses 33–34 he asks:

> Who shall bring a charge against God's elect? It is God who justifies. Who is he who condemns? It is Christ who died, and furthermore is also risen, who is even at the right hand of God, who also makes intercession for us.

Those reproachful thoughts and those condemning feelings come from the "accuser of the brethren" (Revelation 12:10). It is only by confidence in the blood of the Lamb that we can overcome satanic condemnation.

If you've sinned, don't let the devil drive you away from the Lord through condemnation! Instead, confess your sin, and remember, "He is faithful and just to forgive you your sins and to cleanse you from all unrighteousness" (see 1 John 1:9).

DOUBT

The devil sometimes shoots fiery darts of doubt into our minds. He will try to get you to doubt everything from God's existence to your salvation. But his fundamental objective is to cast doubt on the Word of God. An important thing to remember, though, is that there is a difference between the *temptation to doubt* and the *sin of unbelief.* It's possible to be plagued by doubt and yet innocent of the sin of unbelief.

The great English preacher Charles Spurgeon was acutely familiar with this particular form of temptation. He said, "My peculiar temptation has been constant unbelief. I know that God's promise is true. … Yet does this temptation incessantly assail me—'Doubt Him. Distrust Him. He will leave you yet.'"[4] Spurgeon, of course, resisted the temptation, but his statements indicate that he struggled constantly in this area.

So once again I remind you that you are not sinning when you are oppressed by the temptation to doubt. Doubt only becomes sin when it is acted upon and allowed to control us. Satan tempted Eve to doubt God's Word. However, it wasn't until she submitted to his suggestions that she sinned. Just because you're tempted to doubt doesn't mean that you've sinned. You can refuse to give in to those suggestions.

When I was a young Christian, I had heard that certain scholars and theologians questioned the validity of some of the books of the Bible. At that point Satan sought to plant doubt in my mind concerning the Word of God. The thoughts went something like this: "These men are theologians who have studied the Bible for years. They know the Hebrew and the Greek. I know nothing. How can I possibly think I'm right and they're wrong?" Does that sound familiar? Or maybe you've had an experience in which you're reading your Bible and your mind is suddenly flooded with questions like: "Are you sure Jesus Christ even existed?

Could those miracles really have happened? How could someone rise from the dead? What about all the other religions? Isn't it a bit arrogant to think that Jesus is the only way to God?" The list goes on and on.

Satan will suggest these thoughts to you. He is always trying to undermine the Word of God. He tried it with Eve in the Garden, "Has God really said? …" (see Genesis 3:1). He tried it with Jesus in the wilderness, "If You are the Son of God …" (Luke 4:3). You can be sure he'll try it with you. The Word of God is both our compass and rudder to guide us through this stormy Christian life. If the devil can get us to doubt even the smallest truth, he can get us off course. If he can get us to doubt the greater truths, we can end up shipwrecked. That is his goal. Don't give in to doubt. Recognize it as one of the devil's tactics and stand firm on the Word of God.

One last thing—don't confuse honest questions with doubt. Consider the difference between Zacharias' response to the angel Gabriel and Mary's response (Luke 1:18, 34). Both seem-ingly asked the same question, "How shall this be?" It was not the question "How?" but rather the attitude with which the question was posed that differentiated the two. Zacharias asked in unbelief as if to say, "You've got to be kidding? No way!" Mary, on the other hand, was asking in what manner God would accomplish such a wonder. Her humble faith is evidenced in her final statement to Gabriel, "Behold the maidservant of the Lord! Let it be to me according to your word" (Luke 1:38). Mary was not guilty of doubting God's Word; she was submitting to His plan!

There is nothing wrong with asking questions. That's how we learn. Honest questions can turn your temptations to doubt into opportunities to grow in your understanding of the Lord, His Word, and His ways. At the end of every honest question you will find that God is true, even as Paul boasts in Romans 3:4, "Let God be true but every man a liar."

FEAR

Another of the devil's wiles is the use of fear tactics. He threatens evil consequences upon those who would trust and obey the Lord. When the eighteenth century revivalist George Whitefield called upon his friend John Wesley to take over his open-air preaching ministry, Wesley was suddenly struck with the impression that if he were to do so, he would die. Having sought divine guidance by randomly opening his Bible on four different occasions, the Scriptures seemed to confirm his impending death. But those fears proved to be nothing more than the work of the devil seeking to prevent him from entering into the work to which God had called him. It was actually through the acceptance of that invitation that John Wesley entered his evangelistic career, which lasted more than forty years and resulted in the conversion of tens of thousands and the formation of the Methodist Church.

The enemy's fear tactic is vividly seen in the story of Rabbi Leopold Cohn, a Hungarian Jew who through various circumstances came to believe that Jesus is the Messiah of Israel. When he received Christ, he realized that he needed to choose a day on which to make a public confession of his faith by being baptized. His story of the events that transpired on the day of his baptism amply illustrates the devil's attempts to hinder God's work in us through fear. The rabbi said:

> Early that morning, about daybreak, I awakened with a shiver and it seemed as if someone spoke saying, "What are you doing today?"

I sprang out of bed and walked up and down the room like one suffering from high fever almost not knowing what I was doing. I had been anxiously waiting to be baptized as I was looking forward with joy to the time when I could publicly confess the Lord Jesus Christ before men. But now a sudden change came over me. The voice that was talking to me was that of the great enemy of mankind, though of course he was so sly that I could not perceive at the time that it was Satan.

Many questions were proposed to me rapidly one after another and perplexed me so that I felt ill mentally and physically. He questioned thus: "You are going to be baptized, aren't you? Do you know that as soon as you take this step, you will be cut off from your wife whom you love so dearly? She can never live with you again. Do you realize that your four children whom you are so fond of will never call you Papa or look in your face again? Your brothers, sisters, and all your relatives will consider you dead and all their hearts will be broken forever.

"How can you be so cruel to your own flesh and blood? Your own people will despise and hate you more than ever before. You are cutting yourself off from your people. You have no friends in this world. You will be left alone to drift like a piece of timber on the ocean. What will become of your name, your reputation, your official position?"

These thoughts put to me in the form of the most audible questions by Satan, whom I, for the first time, met as a personal enemy, distressed and almost unbalanced my mind. I could not sleep, neither could I eat. My friend who was with me, noticing this, tried to strengthen and encourage me in every possible way, but nothing availed. I knelt down in prayer to God but the satanic delusion was as strong as before.

He continues his story by describing what happened when he conceded defeat to the enemy. Feeling mentally and physically sick, he went to inform the pastor that he would not be able to be baptized. About that same time, another pastor, namely Dr. Andrew Bonar, along with his congregation, felt impressed to pray for this man, knowing he was to be baptized that day. As they began to pray, suddenly the oppression lifted, and instead of canceling his appointment, he was baptized and made his public confession of Christ, just as he had desired to do.

Rabbi Cohn went on to become a powerful witness for the Lord, forming what became known as the American Board of Missions to the Jews. He led many of his fellow Israelites to faith in the Messiah, Jesus.

Did you notice how the devil threatened evil consequences if the rabbi were to obey the Lord? Yet it was nothing more than an idle threat just as it had been with John Wesley. Satan will threaten you just as Saul threatened David, or Tobiah and Sanballat threatened Nehemiah. But that is all he can do because "greater is he that is in you, than he that is in the world" (1 John 4:4 KJV). Again, "If God is for us, who can be against us?" (Romans 8:31).

Don't let the enemy keep you out of the will of God through fear. Remember, "God has not given us a spirit of fear, but of power and of love and of a sound mind" (2 Timothy 1:7). Our heavenly Father has our eternal best in mind. So yield to Him without fear. Watch what He will do. Father knows best.

EVIL THOUGHTS AND IMAGINATIONS

Another manifestation of the "wiles of the devil"

is evil thoughts. Have you ever been in prayer and had your mind suddenly assaulted by blasphemous thoughts? Have you ever been worshipping and had pornographic images flash across your mind? Have you ever gone through a period of time in which your mind was consumed with deplorable thoughts—thoughts that sickened and oppressed you, thoughts that you longed to be delivered from, thoughts of sexual immorality, murder, or suicide? If so, you are not alone. You know firsthand what the apostle Paul was referring to when he spoke of the "fiery darts" or more literally "the flaming arrows" of the wicked one.

An important question to ask at this point is: How can I tell the difference between the flaming arrows of the wicked one and the sin of evil surmising? Evil surmising originates from within, as Jesus said, "Out of the heart proceed evil thoughts" (Matthew 15:19). Evil surmising is within your power to control and has an *element of delight* in it. The flaming arrows of the wicked one, on the other hand, come from outside of you and are, to a certain degree, beyond your power to control. They are also *offensive* to you. You not only do not want to think these thoughts, you consciously reject them.

Another experience from the life of Charles Spurgeon serves as an illustration. Having gone through a prolonged period of blasphemous assaults upon his mind and being near the point of despair, he began questioning even his salvation (after all, how could a true Christian think such thoughts?). He finally confided in an aged godly man who asked him one simple question: "Do you hate these thoughts?" Young Spurgeon replied: "I do." The man replied, "Then they are not yours; … Groan over them, repent of them, and send them on to the devil, the father of them, to whom they belong—for they are not yours."[5]

The devil is subtle; he plants a thought in your mind and wants to make you think it's your thought. But don't own it; instead reject it and realize who is behind it. You can even turn the enemy's weapons back upon him by using those occasions as an opportunity for prayer and worship. You can be like Benaiah who wrested the spear out of the enemy's hand, and killed him with his own spear (2 Samuel 23:21).

> Finally, brethren, whatever things are true, whatever things are noble, whatever things are just, whatever things are pure, whatever things are lovely, whatever things are of good

report, if there is any virtue and if there is anything praiseworthy—meditate on these things.

Philippians 4:8

As nature abhors a vacuum, so our minds cannot long remain empty. Good thoughts leave no room for bad thoughts.

DEPRESSION

Depression is perhaps the most devastating of the "wiles of the devil" inasmuch as the devil gathers up all of the things we've discussed (condemnation, doubt, fear, evil thoughts and imaginations), wraps them in despair, and leaves us with an overwhelming sense of hopelessness.

Many of God's people throughout the ages have known firsthand what it is to be depressed. You might be surprised to find that both the psalmist and the apostle Paul experienced depression. Listen to their words:

In the day of my trouble I sought the Lord; my hand was stretched out in the night without ceasing; my soul refused to be comforted. I remembered God, and was troubled; I complained, and my spirit was overwhelmed. You hold my eyelids open; I am so troubled that I cannot speak.

Psalm 77:2–4

We were burdened beyond measure, above strength, so that we despaired even of life.

2 Corinthians 1:8b

Church history provides many examples as well of those who have suffered from depression. William Cowper, the great English poet and hymn writer, battled manic-depression throughout his life.

Charles Spurgeon said, "I am the subject of depressions of spirit so fearful that I hope none of you ever get to such extremes of wretchedness as I go to."[6]

So we see that God's people are not exempt from depression. Everyone suffers from depression from time to time, some more frequently and more severely than others. The question then is, how do we deal with depression?

First, we need to know what is causing it. There are basically four types of depression. There is depression that is organic in nature (resulting from a bodily malfunction, i.e., hormonal or chemical imbalances). Then there is circumstantial depression; the problems of life have gotten you down. Some depression is directly related to sin. And finally, there is depression that is the direct result of satanic activity.

Determining what type of depression a person is dealing with is not always easy. However, God has promised wisdom for those who ask (James 1:5).

Once we discern the cause, we can proceed with the treatment. If the cause is organic, the treatment will be primarily medical. If the cause is circumstantial, the treatment will be getting a biblical perspective on your circumstances and trusting God. If the cause is sin, repentance is necessary. If the cause is satanic, the spiritual weapons of the Word of God and prayer are the only things that will avail.

Back in the days before there were anti-depressants, William Cowper was prayed out of a deep, dark, suicidal depression by his faithful friend and pastor, John Newton. Although treatment with medications can be beneficial, these treatments should never be used to the exclusion of the Word of God and prayer. It is my opinion that regardless of the root cause of depression, there is a satanic aspect to it. Therefore, I believe that all depression, regardless of its source, should be treated through biblical counseling and intense prayer.

If you have been plagued by depression, remember, "God is faithful, who will not allow you to be tempted beyond what you are able, but with the temptation will also make the way of escape" (1 Corinthians 10:13). Don't believe the devil's lie that your situation is hopeless so you might as well just end it all now. Look to the Lord! Call upon His Name! Stand upon His Word! Pray, and ask others to pray for you. Seek godly counsel from a pastor or a mature Christian friend. Finally, know that "the God of peace will crush Satan under your feet shortly" (Romans 16:20).

Next, we will consider one final aspect of the devil's war against us—*Temptation.*

4 TEMPTATION

> Be sober, be vigilant; because your adversary the devil walks about like a roaring lion, seeking whom he may devour. Resist him, steadfast in the faith, knowing that the same sufferings are experienced by your brotherhood in the world.
>
> *1 Peter 5:8–9*

Satan's most notorious activity is that of tempting mankind. Temptation is the solicitation to do evil and is the common experience of all people, whether they are Christians or not. Yet, Satan puts forth extra effort in tempting Christians. He knows that if he can bring down a Christian, he can, to some degree, discredit the church and bring reproach upon the name of the Lord. As David's sin with Bathsheba gave "great occasion to the enemies of the LORD to blaspheme" (2 Samuel 12:14), so it is with sinning Christians. This is one of Satan's motives for tempting believers.

Another reason Satan will tempt you is simply

because he hates you and wants to destroy you. He knows that "sin, when it is full-grown, brings forth death" (James 1:15).

When Peter referred to Satan as "a roaring lion, seeking whom he may devour," he was no doubt thinking of Satan's activity in tempting man.

Author John Phillips gives us a very graphic picture of what that looks like:

> [Satan] has been studying human nature ever since man was created. Satan helped forge fallen human nature. He is a master psychologist. One person he assails with lusts of the flesh. He has a whole arsenal of darts that can set the senses aflame. Another person he assails with lusts of the eye; someone else with the pride of life. The lust of appetite, the love of applause, and the lure of ambition are among the host of darts Satan uses to kindle fierce fires in our souls.
>
> He knows our weaknesses and strengths. He sends his legions of evil spirits to titillate our senses, inflame our desires, corrupt our souls, weaken our wills, deceive our minds, deaden our consciences, and distort God's truth. Satan has a thousand wiles and he never gives up.[7]

With death and destruction as the aim of the tempter, we cannot afford to take temptation lightly. On the contrary, we must be sober and vigilant in dealing with our adversary, the devil.

RECOGNIZING TEMPTATION

The first thing we need to do in relation to temptation is to learn to recognize when we are being tempted.

One of Satan's attributes is subtlety. He disguises himself so well that quite often the one being tempted is oblivious to his involvement. In other words, Satan doesn't manifest himself to you in all of his hideousness, announcing, "I'm the devil. I'm here to lure you into a trap so I can ultimately destroy you. Now watch me work." No. Instead he hides in the shadows. We don't even realize that he's there behind the scenes, pulling strings and manipulating circumstances.

He oftentimes poses as one who is greatly concerned for our welfare. Recall Eve in the Garden of Eden: Satan suggested to her that God was selfish, that He was holding back something that was good for her.

He used the same approach in the temptation of Jesus. Satan came to Him saying, "Now if You are the Son of God, You shouldn't be starving to death out here. Is that any way for the Son of God to live? Why don't You take these stones over here and turn them into bread? Satisfy Yourself. You deserve it. After all, You're the Son of God."

Like the seasoned angler who knows just the right lure, Satan knows your areas of weakness and tempts you accordingly. He can appear as an angel of light, a damsel in distress, the solution to your financial problems, or the answer to your poor self-image. The list goes on and on. Paul referred to this attribute of Satan when writing to the Corinthians. He said:

> I fear, lest somehow, as the serpent deceived Eve by his craftiness, so your minds may be corrupted from the simplicity that is in Christ.
>
> *2 Corinthians 11:3–4*

Though temptation is sometimes difficult to recognize, you can be sure you are being tempted whenever you are faced with a situation that could lead you to rationalize, compromise, or in any way disobey the Word of God.

AVOIDING TEMPTATION

Another important step in dealing with temptation is making every effort to stay away from it. You can avoid temptation first of all by prayer. Jesus said, "Watch and pray, lest you enter into temptation" (Matthew 26:41).

Second, you can avoid temptation by having a realistic view of yourself. This means recognizing your weaknesses and staying away from those things that pose a special problem for you. If you've had a problem with sexual sin, then you must do everything in your power to avoid any situation that could cause you to stumble. It might mean staying away from a certain person or group of people; it could mean avoiding certain sources of entertainment, such as the Internet, the movies, or the TV, especially cable; or it could mean steering clear of the magazine rack in the local convenience store.

If your past sins have been alcohol or drug related, then you need to avoid people, places, or situations that could lead you into compromise. This same principle applies in every area of weakness. If, after all of this, you still find yourself in a tempting situation, like Joseph when Potiphar's wife threw herself at him, your only recourse is to flee as Joseph did. Knowing your area of vulnerability is actually a step toward victory over temptation.

Remember, "Let him who thinks he stands take heed lest he fall" (1 Corinthians 10:12). Don't put yourself in a tempting situation, but rather, "Flee these things and pursue righteousness, godliness, faith, love, patience, gentleness. Fight the good fight of faith, lay hold on eternal life" (1 Timothy 6:11–12).

OVERCOMING TEMPTATION

The only good news about being tempted is that we are *guaranteed victory over temptation*. It is crucial to know this. Some Christians leave you with the impression that victory is impossible and that backsliding is just another facet of the Christian experience. Yet, nothing could be further from the truth! The Bible tells us that victory is possible. The apostle John said, "My little children, these things I write to you, so that you may not sin" (1 John 2:1). James, in his Epistle, instructs us on how to obtain the victory:

> Therefore submit to God. Resist the devil and he will flee from you. Draw near to God and He will draw near to you.
>
> *James 4:7–8*

Victory begins with total submission to God. If Jesus is not the Lord of our lives, it will be difficult, if not impossible, to be victorious over temptation. Having submitted ourselves to God, we then resist the devil. Resisting the devil means we stand against him with the weapons that God has given to us. Our primary weapon is the Word of God. As we resist, in due time, Satan will flee.

This is beautifully illustrated in the life of Christ in Matthew 4. After fasting for forty days and forty nights, Jesus is met by Satan, who says to Him, "If You are the Son of God, command that these stones become bread" (v. 3). Here our Lord does what we are instructed to do: He resists the devil with the Word of God. "It is written, 'Man shall not live by bread alone, but by every word that proceeds from the mouth of God'" (v. 4).

Each time Satan came with a temptation, Jesus countered with the Word. We are to do the same. When Satan tempts you to revert to your old habits, resist him with 2 Corinthians 5:17, "If anyone is in Christ, he is a new creation; old things have passed away; behold, all things have become new." And with Romans 6:11–12, "Likewise you also, reckon yourselves to be dead indeed to sin, but alive to God in Christ Jesus our Lord. Therefore do not let sin reign in your mortal body, that you should obey it in its lusts."

When Satan tempts you with immorality or substances that are forbidden by God, resist him with 1 Corinthians 6:19–20, "Do you not know that your body is the temple of the Holy Spirit who is in you, whom you have from God, and you are not your own? For you were bought at a price; therefore glorify God in your body and in your spirit, which are God's."

It is in this practical consideration of temptation that we see the divine wisdom of David's statement, "Your word I have hidden in my heart, that I might not sin against You" (Psalm 119:11). Memorized Scripture is a great asset when faced with temptation.

Finally remember:

Our old man was crucified with Him, that the body of sin might be done away with, that we should no longer be slaves of sin … and having been set free from sin, you became slaves of righteousness.

Romans 6:6, 18

No temptation has overtaken you except such as is common to man; but God is faithful, who will not allow you to be tempted beyond what you are able, but with the temptation will also make the way of escape, that you may be able to bear it.

1 Corinthians 10:13

Seeing then that we have a great High Priest who has passed through the heavens, Jesus the Son of God, let us hold fast our confession. For we do not have a High Priest who cannot sympathize with our weaknesses, but was in all points tempted as we are, yet without sin. Let us therefore come boldly to the throne of grace, that we may obtain mercy and find grace to help in time of need.

Hebrews 4:14–16

5

THE ARMOR OF GOD

Therefore take up the whole armor of God, that you may be able to withstand in the evil day, and having done all, to stand. Stand therefore, having girded your waist with truth, having put on the breastplate of righteousness, and having shod your feet with the preparation of the gospel of peace; above all, taking the shield of faith with which you will be able to quench all the fiery darts of the wicked one. And take the helmet of salvation, and the sword of the Spirit, which is the word of God.

Ephesians 6:13–17

Every soldier involved in combat must possess a comprehensive knowledge of the weapons of their warfare. In the passage above, Paul paints for us a picture of a Roman soldier fully dressed for battle, and he uses that picture to explain the various pieces that make up the whole armor of God.

Rather than getting preoccupied with the type of armor that was used by the ancient Romans, we want to concentrate on the message behind the analogy. What exactly is the armor of God?

The armor of God is the eternal truth of God found in the Scriptures. To put on the armor is to apply biblical truth to our lives. Each piece of the armor represents a different aspect of that truth. The armor is necessary to protect us from the attacks of the enemy as we seek to live for the glory of God and advance His kingdom. The belt of truth, the breastplate of righteousness, the boots of peace, the shield of faith, and the helmet of salvation are all, for the most part, defensive, enabling us to stand without losing ground. The sword of the Spirit and prayer are our offensive weapons. We will look first at the defensive aspect of the armor, and then in the next chapter, we will consider the offensive features of the armor.

BELT OF TRUTH

The belt is mentioned first because it is the foundational piece of the armor. It gave the soldier mobility and support. For us, it is the belt of truth. The truths of the Word of God are the foundation from which our warfare is waged. To be girded with the truth means to know the truth and believe it. The enemy cannot be withstood by human reason, tradition, personal charisma, or any other carnal means. God's truth alone must shape our thinking and living.

I'm sure you've noticed that we live in a world full of lies. It's hard to get at the truth today. Do you believe everything you read in the newspapers? I hope not. Unfortunately, for most people truth is not a high priority. Here in the United States we have witnessed a major integrity crisis in the corporate world and among some of our leading politicians, not to mention the day-to-day deceit of one kind or another that we have sadly come to expect. We are actually living in a time when the very concept of truth is being challenged and in some cases openly denied. This makes it all the more important that we as Christians are men and women of truth.

Putting on the belt of truth, then, means knowing THE TRUTH, as well as being ourselves full of integrity. There should be no guile or deceit in us at all.

BREASTPLATE OF RIGHTEOUSNESS

Next, we come to the breastplate of righteousness. The breastplate, of course, protected the vital organs—the heart, the lungs, the pancreas, and the liver. The ancients believed this part of the body to be the seat of the emotions. So we speak of sorrow as being "brokenhearted," or we use the term "bowels of mercy" as a way of describing compassion. Therefore, the breastplate is to protect us in the realm of our emotions. Notice it is the *breastplate* of righteousness. Satan quite often attacks our emotions in regard to righteousness.

We've already talked about condemnation—the feeling that God is against us. When condemnation would overwhelm us, an understanding of the doctrine of the imputed righteousness of Christ serves as our first line of defense. That knowledge is obtained through the Scriptures.

> For He made Him who knew no sin to be sin for us, that we might become the righteousness of God in Him.
>
> *2 Corinthians 5:21*

He made us accepted in the Beloved.

Ephesians 1:6

[That I may] be found in Him, not having my own righteousness … but that which is through faith in Christ, the righteousness which is from God by faith.

Philippians 3:9

Paul was primarily referring to Christ's imputed righteousness when he spoke of being clad with the breastplate of righteousness.

In another sense, putting on the breastplate of righteousness refers to the practice of righteousness. Holy living makes it a lot more difficult for the devil to trip us up. Living right, doing good, and obeying God's commands will be a sure protection against the attacks of the enemy.

BOOTS OF PEACE

We are to have our feet shod with the preparation of the gospel of peace. The Roman soldier wore a studded sandal in battle that gave him security and helped him stand immovable in the conflict. Those shoes gave him confidence. Likewise, the peace of

God gives us security and confidence in battle. It is the peace of God that protects us from discouragement and despair.

But having our feet shod with the preparation of the gospel of peace also speaks of a readiness to share the gospel. As we're out and about in our daily lives—whether at work, out in the community, or on vacation, wherever we go as God's people—we need to be prepared to share the gospel! Do you know the gospel? Are you able to communicate it? Do you see how important it is to learn God's Word, not only for your own benefit, but for the benefit of others as well? The apostle Peter said something similar to what Paul is saying here. He said:

> Sanctify the Lord God in your hearts, and always be ready to give a defense to everyone who asks you a reason for the hope that is in you.
>
> *1 Peter 3:15*

SHIELD OF FAITH

Having considered the belt of truth, the breastplate of righteousness, and the boots of peace, we come now to the shield of faith. The particular shield referred to here was so enormous that the soldier could hide completely behind it. This shield would thoroughly protect him from the barrage of arrows sent by the enemy. What this shield did for the Roman soldier, the shield of faith does for the Christian when we are being bombarded by the flaming arrows of the evil one. The shield of faith is an active trust in the nature, character, love, and promises of God; all of which are made known to us through His Word.

We will never be out of range of Satan's fiery darts. But they can be quenched by the shield of faith. As clever as he is, as vicious as he is, as relentless as he is, we can still have the victory over him through faith, that simple trust in God.

HELMET OF SALVATION

The final piece of defensive equipment is the helmet of salvation. This helmet protects our minds from attacks against the assurance of our salvation. Satan will accuse us of not doing enough for God and then will call into question the validity of our salvation. Understanding and applying the doctrine of salvation by grace alone is certainly one element of what it means to put on the helmet of salvation.

Remember:

> For by grace you have been saved through faith, and that not of yourselves; it is the gift of God, not of works, lest anyone should boast.
>
> *Ephesians 2:8–9*

> Not by works of righteousness which we have done, but according to His mercy He saved us.
>
> *Titus 3:5a*

There is, I believe, another aspect to the helmet of salvation. In writing to the Thessalonians, Paul exhorted them to put on as a *helmet* the hope of salvation (1 Thessalonians 5:8). I think that's also the idea here in Ephesians. What that means practically for Christians is simply that a time is coming when we are going to be gloriously delivered from this present evil world and taken to Heaven! Our future hope is something Paul wanted us to keep at the forefront of our minds. No matter how tough it gets, there is an end in sight. One day the battle will be over and we'll settle down forever with our great King and Savior in His unspeakably glorious kingdom. Remember that, and let that thought spur you on.

SWORD OF THE SPIRIT

We come now to our only offensive weapon and the final piece of armor mentioned in Ephesians chapter 6—the sword of the Spirit, which is the Word of God.

> It is that which God has spoken, His Word, the Bible. It is sharper than any two-edged sword. It is the wisdom of God and the power of God. It commends itself to the reason and conscience. It has the power not only of truth but of divine truth. In opposition to all error, to all false philosophy, to all false principles of morality, to all the fallacies of vice, to all the suggestions of the devil, the sole, simple, and sufficient answer is the Word of God. The Word of God puts to flight all the powers of darkness.
>
> The power of God's Word is accessible for the individual Christian as well as for the Church collectively. All of our triumphs over sin and error are effected by the Word of God. So long as we use the Word of God and rely on it alone, we go on conquering; but when

anything else, be it reason, science, tradition, or the commandments of men is allowed to take its place or to share its office, then the Church, or the Christian, is at the mercy of the adversary.[8]

The Bible is the sword of the Spirit. What does a sword do? A sword enables one to protect himself, or to move offensively against a foe. The Word of God is the weapon the Holy Spirit uses to protect the church, defeat God's foes, and advance His kingdom.

That's why Satan, being the wise strategist that he is, directs his attack at the Word of God. Satan has successfully defeated much of the church by knocking the sword from the church's hand. He's attacked the Bible! Many Christians have lost confidence in the Bible, and have become, in effect, soldiers without weapons. What does a soldier do when he doesn't have a weapon? He runs!

And that's the tragic story of much of the church today; it's running! Instead of moving forward, the church is backpedaling. Instead of boldly proclaiming the eternal Word of the living God, much of the church is cowering in fear and uncertainty. Instead of standing steadfastly upon the truth of the Bible, many in the church are putting their trust in human wisdom and seeking acceptance from the sworn enemies of Christ. Paul says that we are to take up and hold fast the sword of the Spirit, which is the Word of God. Only then are we assured victory.

Now, when Paul spoke of the "word" of God, he used the Greek word *rhema*, not the more familiar Greek word *logos*. *Rhema* is an interesting word that refers to "a saying," or in our context, a particular verse or a number of verses. By using this Greek word, Paul is emphasizing the need to know the Word of God in a detailed manner in order to effectively use it against the devil.

Paul communicates the same idea to Timothy, instructing him to "rightly divide the word of truth" (see 2 Timothy 2:15). The idea is to be able to bring the right word from God to bear upon a given situation. A brief consideration of the earthly ministry of our Lord will enable us to see exactly what Paul is talking about. We have already considered the confrontation between Christ and Satan in the wilderness and have seen how Jesus put Satan to flight with the Word of God. Throughout our Lord's ministry, He repeated this same approach as He dealt with the scribes and the Pharisees.

On each occasion, our Lord's skillful use of the sword of the Spirit silenced His enemies. Take for example the situation recorded in Matthew 21, verses 15 and 16. The religious leaders were angry with Jesus for allowing the children to refer to Him as "Messiah." Do you remember His response? "Have you never read, 'Out of the mouth of babes and nursing infants You have perfected praise'?"

How about the time when the Sadducees posed to Him a hypothetical situation that they thought to be an airtight argument against the resurrection? He responded, "Your mistake is not knowing the Scriptures nor the power of God," and again He said, "Have you not read what was spoken to you by God?" (see Matthew 22:29, 31).

One last example is found in the Lord's response to the Pharisees' assertion that Christ was to be merely the son of David:

> How can they say that the Christ is the Son of David? Now David himself said in the Book of Psalms: "The LORD said to my Lord, ..." therefore David calls Him "Lord"; how is He then his Son?

> *Luke 20:41–44*

In each of these examples, the Captain of our salvation is teaching us indirectly how to effectively wield the sword of the Spirit. Therefore, we must study to show ourselves approved, workmen able to rightly divide and apply the word of truth.

Our ability to effectively use the sword of the Spirit depends upon our knowledge of the Scriptures. Our knowledge of the Scriptures will increase as we spend time reading, meditating, studying, and memorizing them. Here is a quick overview of each of these different approaches to the Word.

Reading

Reading is ordinarily our first and simplest approach to the Scriptures. Perhaps we begin in Genesis and read right through to Revelation. On our way, the Holy Spirit is slowly, but surely reprogramming us and creating in us a Christ-centered worldview. By consistently reading through the Scriptures, we are being trained by the Holy Spirit to think spiritually. The Lord is imparting to us the mind of Christ.

I like to read my Bible in the evenings before going to sleep. It's a great way to end the day. By reading at an average speed for forty-five minutes to an hour each evening, we can get through the entire Bible in less than a year. Once we've finished, we can go back to Genesis and start all over again. The better we know the written Word, the better we'll know the living Word—the Lord Jesus Christ!

Meditation

Meditation is another approach to the Scriptures. Meditation, of course, includes reading, but it is a more analytical approach. The word *meditate* means "to ponder." It means to talk to oneself. That's what we're to do with the Word—think about it and talk to ourselves about it.

Meditating differs from casual reading because it takes more time and greater concentration. When meditating on a portion of Scripture, I'm praying over it and at the same time asking myself questions. To whom was this written? What does it say? How does it apply to me? What are some other Scriptures that relate to what's being said?

When meditating I usually have a pen and notepad handy in order to jot down anything the Lord might impress upon my heart and mind. For me, meditation is best early in the morning and I prefer to meditate on the New Testament. However, each of us has to find our own niche. So find the time that works best for you. The promise of blessing is to the one whose "delight is in the law of the LORD, and in His law he meditates day and night" (Psalm 1:2). Try to spend as much time as you can meditating on the Word. Make it a priority!

Study

Studying the Bible is something that every Christian needs to learn to do. The difference between reading or meditating on the Word and studying the Word would be the use of certain study helps or tools. By tools I mean reference works such as concordances, Bible dictionaries, Bible handbooks, Greek and Hebrew word studies, commentaries, etc. All of these can be very beneficial in our understanding of the Scriptures. If for some reason these types of resources are not available to you, a good study Bible will do.

Another way of fulfilling the need for Bible study is to sit under gifted Bible teachers who teach systematically through the Scriptures. If you have been blessed with this somewhat rare opportunity, I exhort you to thank God and take full advantage of it. In whatever way is best for you, make Bible study a regular part of your life. Rest assured that in doing so you are further equipping yourself with the armor of God.

Memorization

My final bit of advice is to memorize Scripture. Committing the Word of God to memory is indeed a vital part of putting on the whole armor of God. In John's first epistle, chapter 2, verse 4, he states that the strength of the young men who are victorious over the devil stems from the Word of God abiding in them. There is no better way to assure the Word of God is abiding in you than to memorize it.

Start by reading over and over again those Scriptures that speak most powerfully to you. If need be, write them down on a piece of paper and read them over several times each day until they become a part of you. You will find that the Lord will bring those particular verses to mind as powerful resources in your overall arsenal of spiritual weapons.

6 FIT FOR THE FIGHT

> Praying always with all prayer and supplication in the Spirit, being watchful to this end with all perseverance and supplication for all the saints.
>
> *Ephesians 6:18*

The Christian soldier now stands fully dressed for battle. However, he is still not ready to fight. He lacks two essential components of victory—skill and strength. Although a soldier may be equipped with the best weapons, if he lacks skill and strength, victory is uncertain at best. What physical fitness and mental preparedness are to those fighting in the natural realm, prayer is to the Christian soldier. Prayer is the final piece of the Christian soldier's armor. Prayer is the guarantee that the Christian soldier is fit for the fight.

The Scriptures are filled with exhortations to prayer: "Continue steadfastly in prayer" (see Romans 12:12); "Continue earnestly in prayer, being vigilant in it with thanksgiving" (Colossians 4:2); "Pray without ceasing" (1 Thessalonians 5:17).

Prayer is vital. It is essential to victory in our spiritual battle. Yet, it is often forgotten. The neglect of prayer is one of the main reasons for the weakness of many Christians as well as the modern church as a whole. Most Christians and churches do everything but pray! We have obviously failed to understand the importance of prayer.

John Bunyan, who was mentioned earlier, spent thirteen years in prison for preaching the gospel. He said, "You can do more than prayer after you've prayed, but you cannot do more than pray until you have prayed." Spurgeon said, "My heart has no deeper conviction than this, that prayer is the most efficient spiritual agency in the universe next to the Holy Spirit. ... I could as soon think of living without eating or breathing, as living without praying." May God impart to us the same conviction that these men had concerning prayer.

Ephesians 6:18 teaches us five things about prayer in connection with spiritual warfare.

PRAY ALWAYS

First, we are told to pray always. To "pray always" means that throughout the course of the day, over and over again, we are to lift our hearts to God, bringing before Him the issues we're facing. John Wesley described the man who fulfills the injunction to "pray without ceasing":

> His heart is ever lifted up to God at all times and in all places. In this, he is never hindered, much less interrupted by any person or thing. In retirement or company, leisure, business, or conversation his heart is ever with the Lord. Whether he lie down or rise up, God is in all his thoughts. He walks with God continually having the loving eye of his mind still fixed upon Him and everywhere seeing Him that is invisible.

This is what Paul means when he says to pray always.

PRAY IN THE SPIRIT

Next we are to pray in the Spirit. This means to be led by the Spirit in prayer. The way to assure we are praying in the Spirit is to ask the Spirit's assistance as we go to prayer. There's nothing quite as wonderful or thrilling as being empowered by the Holy Spirit in prayer. The heart is impassioned. The mind is clear. Every thought is ordered. Praise, petitions, and intercession flow freely, and one can literally pray for hours, and yet feel that only a few moments have passed. Seek to pray in the Spirit. Spend time asking the Lord to lead before you begin your prayer time. You will find this kind of prayer to be a great adventure and a great faith builder.

Oswald Sanders, former director of the China Inland Mission, said in regards to Spirit-led prayer, "The very fact that God lays a burden of prayer on our hearts and keeps us praying is evidence that He purposes to grant the answer."

When asked if he really believed that the two men for whom he had prayed for more than fifty years would be converted, George Müeller replied, "Do you think that God would have kept me praying all these years if He did not intend to save them?" This is Spirit-led prayer.

WATCHFUL IN PRAYER

After praying in the Spirit, the next exhortation is

to be watchful in prayer. Be alert. Be on your guard. Pay attention and be ready always to do battle in prayer. Is the Lord moving? Pray! Is the enemy attacking? Pray! Has a fellow soldier fallen? Pray! Set a vigil! Get a prayer partner! Pray! Pray! Pray!

PERSEVERANCE IN PRAYER

From watchfulness, we move on to perseverance in prayer. Have you ever prayed about something and felt like no one was listening? Time and time again, you have brought your request before the Lord and yet nothing changes. What do you do then? If you are like most people, you will be tempted to just give up. Don't do that! Jesus taught a parable about a woman pestering a judge until he heeded her request with the intention of exhorting us always to pray and not lose heart (Luke 18:1–8).

When we don't see immediate answers to our prayers, we tend to want to give up. That's when we need perseverance. Effective praying is like running a marathon. Endurance is the key. Do you remember the wonderful promise Jesus made concerning prayer? "Ask, and it will be given to you; seek, and you will find; knock, and it will be opened to you" (Matthew 7:7).

What most people fail to realize is that this is a conditional promise. Unfortunately, the condition is missed in most of our English translations. The condition is perseverance. A literal rendering of the Greek text reads, "Keep on asking, keep on seeking, keep on knocking." How many times have we failed to receive an answer to our prayers because we have failed to meet the condition of perseverance?

One of the greatest obstacles to perseverance in prayer was evident in the apostles themselves. Jesus said of them, "The spirit indeed is willing, but the flesh is weak" (Matthew 26:41). To persevere in prayer takes commitment, discipline, and self-sacrifice.

Can you imagine how many times George Müeller must have felt like giving up during those fifty years of praying for the salvation of his two friends? But he was committed, and we must also be committed if we expect to see the enemy vanquished, God's work flourish, and souls brought to Christ. Persevere in prayer. "You who make mention of the LORD, do not keep silent, and give Him no rest till He establishes and till He makes Jerusalem a praise in the earth" (Isaiah 62:6–7).

SUPPLICATION FOR ALL THE SAINTS

The final word on prayer in Ephesians 6:18 is supplication for all the saints. Praying for God's people is a privilege that each of us possesses. Are you looking for a ministry? Do you desire to serve the Lord, but have yet to discover your calling? Make this your work for the kingdom—pray for the church.

Pray for your pastor and all pastors who are genuinely seeking to serve the Lord. Pray for the gospel of Christ. Pray for those serving the Lord as missionaries. Pray for all of God's servants who are serving the body of Christ in some way.

Pray also for God's people who go out daily into the secular world that they would be filled with the Spirit. Pray that they would be the salt of the earth and the light of the world. Pray for the sick and suffering among God's people. You can have a worldwide ministry and never leave your own city limits by making supplication for all the saints.

Too many people underestimate the power of prayer. God uses the prayers of ordinary people in their own homes to vitally affect and bless His ministries. A wonderful example of the power of prayer is evidenced in the testimony of Hudson Taylor, a missionary to China and founder of the China Inland Mission.

Some years ago, the record of a wonderful work of grace in connection with one of the stations of the China Inland Mission attracted a good deal of attention. Both the number and spiritual character of the converts had been far greater than at other stations where the consecration of the missionaries had been just as great. This rich harvest of souls remained a mystery until Hudson Taylor, on a visit to England, discovered the secret.

At the close of one of his addresses, a gentleman came forward to make his acquaintance. In the conversation that unfolded, Mr. Taylor was surprised at the intimate knowledge the man possessed about that particular mission station. "But how is it," Mr. Taylor asked, "that you are so conversant with the conditions of that work?" "Oh!" he replied, "The missionary there and I are old college mates: for years we have regularly corresponded; he has sent me names of inquirers and converts and these I have daily taken to God in prayer." At last the secret was found—a praying man, praying definitely, praying daily.

Prayer is the great spiritual exercise that makes one "fit for the fight."

CONCLUSION

Paul, in his writings to the Corinthians, said that he was not ignorant of Satan's devices (2 Corinthians 2:11). Neither can we be ignorant of Satan's devices. It has been my intention in this book not only to reveal our enemy's character and devices, but also to guide you in the appropriation of the victory that God has given us over him.

We have considered Satan's kingdom as well as his activity in the world and his assault upon God's people. Although he is crafty, intelligent, and well armed, he is powerless against a Christian who is fortified with the whole armor of God and spiritually fit through prayer. Understanding these truths is useless unless we apply what we've learned to our daily walk of faith. And the spiritual principles from God's Word can only be acted upon through the power of the Holy Spirit.

Ask God to fill you with His Spirit and to lead you on to victory. You can be sure He will.

Finally, my brethren, be strong in the Lord and in the power of His might.

Ephesians 6:10

81

NOTES

[1] Lewis, C.S. *Screwtape Letters* (San Francisco, CA: HarperCollins, 2001), p. IX.

[2] For more information on religious beliefs, go to Barna Research Online (http://www.barna.org/cgi-bin/PagePressRelease.asp?PressReleaseID=92&Reference=B).

[3] Bunyan, John. *Grace Abounding to the Chief of Sinners.* URL: www.johnbunyan.org/text/bun-abounding.htm (January 23, 2004).

[4] Spurgeon, C.H. (November 17, 1861). "The Roaring Lion." URL: http://www.spurgeongems.org/vols7-9/chs419.pdf (November 3, 2003).

[5] Spurgeon, C.H. (January 8, 1860). "The King's Highway Opened and Cleared." URL: http://www.spurgeon.org/sermons/0293.htm (November 3, 2003).

[6] Spurgeon, C.H. (May 20, 1866). "Joy and Peace in Believing." URL: http://www.spurgeongems.org/vols10-12/chs692.pdf (November 3, 2003).

[7] Phillips, John. *Exploring Ephesians & Philippians* (Grand Rapids, MI: Kregel Publications, 1993), p. 196–197.

[8] Hodge, Charles. *Ephesians* (Carlisle, PA; Banner of Truth, 1998), p. 287.

ABOUT THE AUTHOR

Brian Brodersen has been involved in pastoral ministry since 1981. He served as senior pastor of Calvary Chapel Vista, California, and also as senior pastor of Calvary Chapel Westminster, London, England.

Brian has been extensively involved in missionary work throughout Europe. He now serves as the associate pastor to Chuck Smith at Calvary Chapel of Costa Mesa, California.

Brian and his wife Cheryl have four children and two grandsons and reside in Southern California.

If you have questions or would like more information regarding Pastor Brian's ministry, please call the following numbers:

US: 714.979.4422

UK: +44 (0)20 8466 5365

You may also go to the following Web site for information:

www.backtobasicsradio.com

OTHER BOOKS AVAILABLE

Consuming Fire
The Hope of Revival Among the Nations

ISBN: 978-1-93166-770-8

For thus says the High and Lofty One: "I dwell in the high and holy place, with him who has a contrite and humble spirit, to revive the spirit of the humble, and to revive the heart of the contrite ones."

Isaiah 57:15

In *Consuming Fire,* Pastor Brian Brodersen reminds us that throughout history, God's patience has been a defining characteristic of His interaction with mankind. The revivals of the past show that not only has He been reluctant to judge, He has delighted in showing mercy! If you long to experience personal revival, Pastor Brian shows that it is guaranteed to those who follow God's blueprint found in the Scriptures.

The Gifts of the Holy Spirit

978-0-97002-181-6

What are the gifts of the Spirit?

There is probably no greater area of ignorance within the church today than in the area of spiritual gifts. Drawing from Scripture, Pastor Brian provides solid biblical insight into the gifts and power of the Holy Spirit and how they are at work in the church today.

Caught Up!

978-0-97002-182-3

Just what is the Rapture?

In a straightforward, easy-to-understand style, Pastor Brian provides a solid biblical foundation for the doctrine of the Rapture. Your heart will be encouraged as you read of the plan that God has for those who have put their trust in Jesus Christ.

Who Do You Say that I Am?
The Uniqueness of Jesus

ISBN: 978-1-93166-785-2

Jesus ... said to them, "But who do you say that
I am?"

Matthew 6:15

WHO IS JESUS?

WHAT MAKES HIM UNIQUE?

WHY DID HIS BIRTH, LIFE, DEATH, AND
RESURRECTION FOREVER ALTER HISTORY?

Peter answered and said, "The Christ of God."

Luke 9:20

Each of us must answer this all-important question:
Who do you say that Jesus is? What will your response
be? Just another man? A prophet? Or will you answer
as Peter did, "The Christ of God"?

WHO DO YOU SAY THAT I AM?

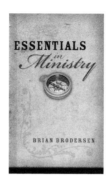

Essentials of Ministry
ISBN: 978-1-15975-033-2

Ministry in today's world is a mixed bag of many styles, models, and viewpoints. Some ministry models are taken from the business world, while others from current postmodern mind-sets. The question the pastor or Christian worker should ask himself or herself is not, "Do these ministry models work?" but "Are they biblical?"

Essentials in Ministry takes a much-needed look at the core areas of ministry and includes a practical and peaceful answer to the Emergent and Church Growth debates. You will also find the answers to such questions as: "What are the essential components of ministry?" and "What is the church supposed to look like today?"

Excellence in Ministry
ISBN: 978-1-15975-043-1

Excellence in Ministry is a practical guide to fruitful, pastoral ministry.

We who are in the ministry ought to endeavor to do church in such a way that brings glory to God and helps as many people as possible to become disciples of Jesus Christ. Some of the questions addressed in this book are:

- Have you been called into the ministry?
- What is the task of the pastor?
- How is a person equipped for the work?

A companion to *Essentials in Ministry*, this book is for those who are starting out in ministry or ready to give up. May it encourage you to stay the course and enable you to produce much fruit for the kingdom.